Guile's of the Devil

TM Brooks

Dedication

It would take a full book to acknowledge all who have helped me, fed me the word, held me accountable to my actions, tried to guide me on the right path. So I'll start on the beginning of my life with the Lord.

To my wife Karen who is enjoying fellowship with the Lord in person. (miss you baby) There are not enough words in the human language to describe how much I love you for picking me. God orchestrated the perfect woman for me. Thank you Lord for using her to bring me to the deliverance of Jesus Christ and for staying the course with me through all my setbacks and pitfalls. And for always encouraging me in my passion to write down the words the Lord gave & gives to me in the writing of my poems, songs and scribblings like this.

To my Pastor & friend Raul Montano. Thank you for your patience, rebukes and guidance in helping me stay on track with Jesus Christ and picking me up when I fall. (literally:) The times we sat quietly sharing some of our pasts encounters in life. Those times are more precious to me than you may know. For giving me insights in doing this (I don't know what to call it) book? Helpful hints in how Satan attacks? Study Guide? To my children (all of you) and family from day one I have loved you and pray for you with all my heart.

And to my church family at Refuge Bible Fellowship, you must know how much I love you all! Remember my motto....

LIFE IS AN ADVENTURE!

(Best experienced with God by your side.)

Keep the full Armor of God on at all times.

Ephesians 6:10-13

"Finally, be strong in the Lord and in the strength of His might.

Put on the whole armor of God, that you may be able to stand against the schemes of the devil. For we do not wrestle against flesh and blood, but against the rulers, against the authorities, against the cosmic powers over this present darkness, against spiritual forces of evil in the heavenly places. Therefore, take up the whole armor of God, that you may be able to withstand in the evil day, and having done all to stand firm."

There may be some reading this that may not have asked the Lord Jesus Christ to be your Savior. This little prayer is just for you. God loves you and will never fail you. He wants to walk with you for all eternity.

Lord Jesus, please forgive me of my sins, I believe that you died for me and rose again and that you forgive all those that confess and repent.

So I am asking your forgiveness for my sins.

He is faithful to His Word.

Acknowledgment

To my friend & Pastor

Raul Montano for your support and suggestions, thank you

To my daughter Jamnia for your support and suggestions, thank you

To Nick & Andrea M for the hours/days/weeks/months helping get things in order and making sure this old man stays well fed.

To my extended family Imre & Laura Borcsa, thank you for your love and support. Give the glory to God!

To Kevin, owner of Darkstar Tattoos for his remarkable cover design

To Casper my publishing project manager for his patience and understanding in my constant questioning and changes, thank you for your understanding

Table of Content

Page Blank Intentionally

"Guile's of The Devil"

PROVERBS 16:1-3 1. The plans of the heart belong to man, but the answer of the tongue is from the Lord. 2. All the ways of man are pure in his own eyes, but the Lord weighs the spirit. Commit your work to the Lord, and your plans will be established.

Guile's of The Devil

This is intended to be a guide for how to stand firm in the Lord, and what to look for when Satan tries to attack you.

And if you are of the Christian Belief and walking in the faith of Jesus Christ as I am, make no mistake, Satan will make every effort, and use whatever means he has at his disposal to distract you from your walk with God!

And as my Pastor and friend Raul Montano reminded me of at a dinner fellowship with he and his wife, a book the leaders group did a study and review of (a good book to read by the way) by Warren W. Wiersbe "The Strategy of Satan".

I have read a few books on the evil ways that Satan attacks, and believe me when I say, the best book to read on this subject on a daily basis is "The Bible". The other books help to give insight, understanding and a clear view of who Satan is. And reviewing them after dinner I found that they all for the most part focus to some degree on Satan going straight to the mind to place wicked thoughts and temptations, and primarily works on your pride.

We know we can't rely on what we ("feel") in our hearts.

God tells us in the word in Jeremiah 17:9-10;

9 The heart is deceitful above all things, and desperately sick; who can understand it? 10 "I the Lord search the heart and test the mind, to give every man according to his ways, according to the fruit of his deeds."

Satan can get in your mind and lead you astray, only if you let him.

Be strong in the word of God & rely on the strength of the Lord!

Guile's of the Devil

CHAPTER ONE

NOTES

Who is Satan

As described by Wikipedia;

A devil is the personification of evil as conceived in various cultures and religious traditions. It is seen as the objectification of a hostile and destructive force. (Fails to recognize there is only one devil,)

First of all, how many religions are there estimated to be?

It is estimated that there are over 4,200 different religions, denominations, religious bodies, faith groups, tribes, cultures, movements, ultimate concerns, ideologies, and cults, which at some point in the future will be countless.

Why is this important to know?

Because there is only one true God, and humankind needs to discern who that one true God is. And how is it possible? By going to the source (the beginning): The Creator of all things, God! After delving into the deviousness of Satan, I will follow up with the second half.

How does Satan deceive!

Satan, depicted as a powerful and cunning figure in various religions and beliefs, is known to employ numerous tactics to deceive individuals.

While interpretations may vary depending on religious beliefs, here are some common ways in which Satan is said to deceive:

5

CHAPTER TWO

NOTES

1. **Temptation:** Satan is often associated with tempting people to stray from their moral or spiritual path (as Christians, we know Satan is directly responsible for this). He entices us as individuals with promises of power, pleasure, or material wealth, exploiting our desires and weaknesses. He employs various means to accomplish his goals of temptation, which will be touched upon further in this manuscript.
2. **False teachings:** Satan spreads false doctrines, beliefs, or ideologies that distort the truth and lead people astray from the path of righteousness. By distorting or misrepresenting religious or spiritual teachings, he sows confusion and creates divisions.
3. **Manipulation of perception:** Satan is known to manipulate perceptions and sow doubt in people's minds. By distorting reality or appearing as an angel of light, he can deceive individuals into making harmful choices or embracing false beliefs.
4. **Exploiting vulnerabilities:** Satan preys on human vulnerabilities, such as fear, pride, and insecurity. He uses these weaknesses to manipulate individuals and lead them away from their intended spiritual or moral journey.
5. **Disguise:** Satan is often portrayed as a master of disguise, able to take on different forms or appear as something or someone desirable to deceive individuals. This ability allows him to masquerade as something harmless or even beneficial, concealing his true intentions.
6. **Division and discord:** Satan will always make every effort to exploit the many differences among people, promoting discord, hatred, and conflict. By fueling animosity and fostering a sense of superiority or self-righteousness, he can lead individuals and communities away from love, unity, fellowship, and understanding.

CHAPTER THREE

The beliefs depicted in these writings are derived from the (**The Holy Bible**

- The truth of God's Word). Different faiths and belief systems may have varying understandings of Satan and his methods of deception. Some self-proclaimed Christian churches do not believe in the deity of Christ and even disbelieve that Satan exists, yet still, call themselves Christians. It is the belief of this writer that there is only one true God. Our Father in heaven, Jesus Christ, and the Holy Spirit constitute that one true God.

How Does Satan Manipulate The Truth?

Satan is often associated with manipulating the truth to deceive individuals. Here are some ways in which Satan has managed or manages to manipulate the truth:

NOTES

1. **Half-truths:** Satan may mix elements of truth with falsehoods to create a distorted version of reality. By presenting partial truths, he can manipulate individuals into accepting a false narrative or belief system.

2. **Distortion and misinterpretation:** Satan may twist the meaning or intent of true teachings or scriptures. By selectively emphasizing certain aspects and ignoring others, he can lead individuals to adopt a skewed understanding(s) of the truth.

Does the phrase taken out of context ring a bell?

3. **False miracles and signs:** Satan has the ability to perform deceptive miracles or signs, creating an illusion of authenticity. These false demonstrations of power can confuse individuals and make them more susceptible to accepting lies as truth.

4. **Manipulation of emotions and perceptions:** Satan can exploit human emotions, biases, and cognitive biases to manipulate how individuals perceive and interpret the truth. By playing on fears, desires, or preconceived notions, he can lead people to embrace false beliefs or reject genuine truths.

5. **Counterfeit spiritual experiences:** Satan can and does create counterfeit spiritual experiences that mimic genuine encounters with the divine. These experiences can be designed to mislead individuals into following false teachings or embracing deceptive ideologies.

6. **Influencing human authorities:** Satan can and does exert influence over human leaders, authorities, and influential figures. By manipulating those in positions of power, he can shape societal narratives and propagate false information.

It's important to remember that these explanations are rooted in true biblical Christian beliefs and may not align with all belief systems or perspectives. Different faiths and individuals may have varying interpretations of how Satan manipulates the truth or even if Satan truly exists. **The Bible is very clear that Satan is real. Eph. 6:11**

13

CHAPTER FOUR

How does Satan appeal to desires?

Satan often exploits human desires as a means to deceive individuals.

Here are some ways, but not all-inclusive, in which Satan works in appealing to desires:

NOTES

1. **Promising power and control:** Satan offers individuals the promise of power, authority, or control over their circumstances. By tapping into the desire for dominance or influence, he can tempt people into making choices that compromise their values or moral principles.

2. **Appealing to material wealth:** Satan entices individuals with the allure of wealth, luxury, and material possessions. By exploiting the desire for financial security or abundance, he can tempt people to prioritize worldly possessions over spiritual or ethical considerations.

3. **Fostering pride and self-importance:** Satan plays human pride, encouraging individuals to pursue recognition, status, and a sense of superiority. By fueling the desire for personal glory and elevating oneself above others, he can lead people away from humility and compassion.

4. **Exploiting sensual desires:** Satan tempts individuals with the pursuit of pleasure, sensual gratification, and indulgence in physical desires. By appealing to human appetites and passions, he can lead people astray from self-discipline, moderation and their walk with God.

5. **Offering shortcuts and instant gratification:** Satan presents shortcuts or quick fixes to fulfill desires or achieve goals. By tempting individuals with the allure of immediate satisfaction, he can and does lead them to bypass the necessary steps or compromises required for long-term growth or genuine fulfillment.

6. **Exploiting insecurities and fears:** Satan preys on human insecurities, fears, and vulnerabilities. By exploiting feelings of inadequacy or fear of rejection, he can manipulate individuals into seeking validation, acceptance, or security through means that contradict their values or principles.

17

CHAPTER FIVE

What kind of disguises does Satan use?

Satan is often portrayed as employing various disguises or deceptive appearances to deceive individuals. While specific descriptions may vary, here are some common disguises associated with Satan:

NOTES

1. **Angel of light:** One of the most commonly mentioned disguises is that of an angel of light. In this form, Satan presents himself as a benevolent and divine being, appearing radiant and pure. This disguise allows him to gain trust and lead people astray by presenting false teachings or misleading guidance.

2. **Serpent or snake:** Satan is depicted as appearing in the form of a serpent or snake. This disguise refers to the story of the Garden of Eden in which Satan, in the guise of a serpent, tempts Eve into disobeying God's command.

3. **Human form:** Satan is believed to have the ability to take on a human appearance, blending in with ordinary people. By assuming a human guise, he can easily interact with individuals and manipulate them without raising suspicion.

4. **Tempting figures:** Satan may take on the guise of an appealing or desirable figure, tailored to exploit specific weaknesses or desires. This could involve appearing as a seductive lover, a charismatic leader, or an influential authority figure.

5. **Deceptive voices:** Satan is sometimes associated with whispering deceptive thoughts or suggestions into the minds of individuals. These whispered voices can be subtle and may mimic one's own thoughts, making it difficult to discern their true origin.

6. **Religious leaders or figures:** In religious contexts, Satan may masquerade as a religious leader or a revered figure within a faith. By adopting this disguise, he can manipulate religious doctrines, sow discord, and lead followers away from a true walk with God.

21

CHAPTER SIX

How does Satan create doubt?

Satan is often associated with creating doubt in order to undermine faith, beliefs, and trust in God. Here are some ways in which Satan is believed to create doubt:

NOTES

1. **Questioning the truth:** Satan raises doubts about the validity and reliability of biblical or spiritual teachings. By prompting individuals to question the authenticity or relevance of their beliefs, he sows seeds of uncertainty.

2. **Challenging the character of God or deities:** Satan attempts to distort or malign the character of God, presenting Him as unjust, uncaring, or unreliable. By casting doubt on the wisdom and power of God, he can undermine faith and trust in the divine guidance of our Lord.

3. **Highlighting perceived inconsistencies or contradictions:** Satan draws attention to perceived inconsistencies or contradictions within the bible, doctrines, or practices. By focusing on apparent discrepancies, he can create doubt and confusion about the coherence and reliability of biblical teachings.

4. **Exploiting unanswered questions and mysteries:** Satan uses unresolved questions, mysteries, or gaps in understanding to foster doubt. By highlighting the limits of human knowledge or the absence of definitive answers, he can and does provoke uncertainty and skepticism.

5. **Appealing to human reasoning and skepticism:** Satan exploits human skepticism and reliance on reason by emphasizing the need for empirical evidence or logical proofs. By encouraging individuals to reject faith in favor of tangible evidence, he creates doubt about the existence or relevance of God.

6. **Targeting personal weaknesses and insecurities:** Satan exploits personal doubts, insecurities, and vulnerabilities. By magnifying feelings of inadequacy, guilt, or unworthiness, he can and does undermine self-confidence and belief in one's worthiness of God's grace or guidance.

25

CHAPTER SEVEN

How does Satan distort scriptures?

According to some theologian scholars, Satan is believed to distort scripture to mislead and deceive individuals. We, as Christians know this to be true just by reading the scripture in the Bible. Here are some ways in which Satan distorts scriptures:

NOTES

1. **Misquoting or altering:** Satan may deliberately misquote or alter passages from Bible texts to change their intended meaning. By manipulating the words or context, he can lead people to embrace false interpretations or beliefs.

2. **Cherry-picking verses:** Satan selectively emphasizes certain verses while disregarding others, thereby distorting the overall message of the scripture. By focusing on isolated passages, he can present a skewed understanding that aligns with his deceptive agenda.

3. **Twisting the context:** Satan manipulates the context in which scriptural passages are presented. By taking verses out of their historical, cultural, or theological context, he can and does distort their original intent and mislead individuals.

4. **Adding or subtracting from the text:** Satan may introduce additional texts or teachings that are not originally part of the scripture. Conversely, he may also attempt to remove or downplay significant portions of the text, altering the overall message and distorting the truth. Writing new bibles?

5. **Ignoring the intended audience:** Satan disregards the original audience or cultural context for which the scriptures were intended. By failing to consider the specific cultural, historical, or linguistic nuances, he can misinterpret the intended message and lead people astray.

6. **Promoting personal interpretations:** Satan may encourage subjective and self-serving interpretations of scriptures. By promoting individualistic or relativistic interpretations, he can lead people away from the original understanding of the text.

29

CHAPTER EIGHT

How does Satan influence human authorities?

Satan is believed to exert influence over human authorities and leaders. The sin within us is like an open door. It's like walking into a fast-food restaurant, and the counter person says welcome, not knowing if the person is coming in to rob them or go on a shooting spree. Here are some ways in which Satan is said to influence human authorities:

NOTES

1. **Corruption and manipulation:** Satan tempts and manipulates those in positions of power, exploiting their vulnerabilities, desires, and ambitions. By appealing to their self-interest or feeding their ego, he can influence their decisions and actions to serve his deceptive purposes.

2. **Promotion of worldly values:** Satan can and most likely does encourage human authorities to prioritize worldly values such as wealth, power, and fame over spiritual or ethical considerations. By fostering a mindset focused on material gain and personal gain, he can sway their decisions away from principles of justice, compassion, and integrity.

3. **Division and conflict:** Satan is associated with promoting discord, division, and conflict among human authorities. By fueling animosity, pride, and competition, he creates a climate of hostility and hinders cooperation for the greater good.

4. **False ideologies and doctrines:** Satan inspires and influences human authorities to embrace and propagate false ideologies or doctrines that align with his deceptive agenda. By distorting the truth, promoting harmful beliefs, or encouraging oppressive practices, he can corrupt the decision-making processes of authorities.

5. **Exploiting fear and insecurity:** Satan may manipulate human authorities by playing on their fears and insecurities. By exploiting their concerns about loss of power, reputation, or control, he can influence them to make decisions based on self-preservation rather than the well-being of those they govern.

6. **Blinding them to the truth:** Satan is believed to blind human authorities to the truth, preventing them from recognizing or accepting divine guidance or higher moral principles. By clouding their judgment and obscuring their perception, he can lead them astray from wise and just decision-making.

CHAPTER NINE

NOTES

How does Satan use demons?

According to Christian beliefs, Satan is often depicted as having influence over demons and using them to carry out his deceptive agenda. Here are some ways in which Satan is said to use demons:

1. **Temptation and manipulation:** Demons are believed to be agents of Satan who actively tempt and manipulate individuals. They may influence human thoughts, emotions, and desires to lead them away from righteousness and towards sinful actions or beliefs.

2. **Deception and false teachings:** Demons are associated with spreading false teachings, ideologies, and doctrines that distort the truth and lead people astray. They may disseminate misleading information, create confusion, and promote deceptive practices to undermine faith and spiritual growth.

3. **Possession and oppression:** Demonic possession occurs when a demon takes control of a person's body or mind, causing them to exhibit abnormal behavior or experience torment. Satan is believed to use possession as a means to disrupt lives, sow chaos, and weaken the faith of individuals.

4. **Inflicting harm and suffering:** Demons are often associated with causing physical, mental, and emotional harm to individuals. They may bring about illness, torment, or spiritual bondage, leading people to question their beliefs or lose hope.

5. **Spiritual warfare:** Satan is believed to employ demons as soldiers in a spiritual battle against the forces of good. They engage in spiritual warfare by attacking believers, hindering their spiritual growth, and attempting to lead them away from their faith.

6. **Influence over supernatural phenomena:** Demons are often associated with supernatural phenomena such as hauntings, poltergeists, and paranormal activities. It is believed that Satan can use these phenomena to create fear, confusion, and doubt in individuals, furthering his deceptive purposes.

CHAPTER TEN

What are the names used by Satan?

In Christianity and various religions and traditions, Satan is associated with different names or titles that are used to refer to him. Here are some of the commonly used names or titles for Satan:

NOTES

1. **Satan:** This is the most widely recognized name for the angel associated with evil and deception. It is derived from Hebrew and means "adversary" or "opposer."

2. **Lucifer:** This name is often used to refer to Satan before his fall from grace. It comes from Latin and means "light-bringer" or "morning star." The name is associated with the pride and rebellion that led to Satan's downfall.

3. **Beelzebub:** This name, which originates from Hebrew and means "Lord of the Flies," is often used as a title for Satan. It emphasizes his role as a chief demon or ruler of other demonic forces.

4. **Devil:** This term comes from the Greek word "diabolos," meaning "accuser" or "slanderer." It is used to refer to Satan as the embodiment of evil and the enemy of God.

5. **The Serpent:** In the biblical context of the Garden of Eden, Satan is depicted as the serpent who tempts Eve to disobey God's command. The term "serpent" is often used metaphorically to refer to Satan.

6. **The Dragon:** This imagery is often associated with Satan, symbolizing his power, ferocity, and evil nature. The dragon is depicted as a monstrous creature, representing chaos and destruction.

7. **The Evil One:** This phrase is used to describe Satan as the epitome of evil and wickedness. It emphasizes his role as the source of temptation, deceit, and malevolence.

41

CHAPTER ELEVEN

Is Satan a fallen angel?

Yes, according to many religious beliefs, Satan is regarded as a fallen angel. The concept of Satan as a fallen angel originates primarily from the Abrahamic religions, including Judaism, Christianity, and Islam. Here is a brief explanation of this belief:

NOTES

1. **In Christianity:** According to Christian teachings, Satan was originally an angel created by God who rebelled against God's authority. He, Satan, along with other rebellious angels, a third of them according to Rev.12:9, was cast out of heaven and became a fallen angel. The narrative of Satan's fall is often associated with the pride and desire for power that led him to oppose God.

2. **In Judaism:** While Jewish beliefs about Satan vary, some interpretations within Judaism also consider Satan as a fallen angel. The concept of Satan as a rebellious angel who opposes God's will can be found in certain Jewish texts and interpretations.

3. **In Islam:** In Islamic theology, Satan is believed to be a jinn (a supernatural creature) rather than an angel. However, similar to the concept of a fallen angel, Islamic teachings describe Satan as a creature who defied God's command and was banished from the heavens due to his disobedience. Taking with him a third of the angelic population.

45

CHAPTER TWELVE

What does the Holy Bible say about the origin and subsequent fall of Satan, and does he have a name as the angel.

The Holy Bible, God's truth, His infallible word, provides insights into the origin and fall of Satan, though the details are not extensive. Here are some key passages that are often referenced:

NOTES

1. **Ezekiel 28:12-17:** This passage is addressed to the king of Tyre but is often interpreted metaphorically to describe the fall of Satan. It speaks of a "cherub" who was created as a guardian angel but became prideful, leading to his downfall.

2. **Isaiah 14:12-15:** This passage is a lamentation against the king of Babylon, but it is also associated with Satan's fall. + It portrays the pride and rebellion of a figure referred to as "Day Star, son of Dawn" or "Lucifer," who sought to exalt himself above God but was cast down.

3. **In Luke 10:18,** "I saw Satan fall like lightning from Heaven".

4. **Genesis 3:5** Satan's temptation of Eve.

5. **Job 1:12-19; 2:7** Satan's work as a destroyer.

6. **2 Cor. 11:14** Satan's masquerading as an "Angel of Light."

While these passages provide descriptions of Satan's fall, they do not offer a comprehensive account of his origin or the events leading to his rebellion.

The Bible does not explicitly provide a specific name for Satan as an angel before his fall. The name "Lucifer" is derived from the Latin translation of the Hebrew word in Isaiah 14:12.

<u>The question that I ponder is how could Satan even hope to dethrone/fight God? Is it Pride blinding him from reality. Satan needs permission from God to affect His people. What's that tell you of Satan's power against God?</u>

49

CHAPTER THIRTEEN

NOTES

How many angels fell from heaven?

The exact number of angels who are believed to have fallen from heaven is not specified in the Bible. The Bible does mention the rebellion of a group of angels led by Satan, but it does not provide a specific count of the fallen angels other than a third. The focus of the biblical narrative is typically on the fallen angel known as Satan or the devil rather than on enumerating the precise number of fallen angels, just that a third was swept down. The Bible does not provide a specific percentage or numerical count of the angels who fell from heaven. The Bible generally does not delve into precise numbers or percentages when discussing angelic beings or the fall of angels. The emphasis is typically on conveying spiritual truths and moral lessons rather than providing specific quantitative details. Therefore, any specific percentage or numerical count of fallen angels would be speculative and not derived from biblical sources.

Does the bible say anywhere about a third of the angels fell from heaven?

Yes, God speaks of a third of the angels falling from heaven, as mentioned in the Bible. The reference can be found in the Book of Revelation, specifically in Revelation 12:1-12. The passage describes a great red dragon (often referred to as Satan or the devil) who sweeps a third of the stars out of the sky and throws them to the earth. Stars represent angels in biblical symbolism, so this verse is understood by theologians to refer to a third of the angels rebelling and falling with Satan.

53

CHAPTER FOURTEEN

NOTES

Revelation 12:4 (ESV version) states:

"His tail swept down a third of the stars of heaven and cast them to the earth. And the dragon stood before the woman who was about to give birth so that when she bore her child, he might devour it."

Is the bible considered to be the truth?

The Bible is known to be the very word of God breathed into the scribes or Apostles, men to be read, learned and its Gospel is to be spread to the ends of the earth. (To all the nations or across all the nations)

Many religious believers of various doctrines believe it (the Bible) to be a sacred text and a source of spiritual truth. However, opinions on the nature and interpretation of truth can vary among different individuals and religious traditions (False Doctrines)

But for those who adhere to the beliefs of a particular faith (Christianity), the Bible contains the true Word of God, His divine revelations and teachings that are essential for understanding God's will and His (God's) moral principles.

Outside of religious faith, the Bible is also recognized as an important historical and literary document that provides insights into ancient cultures and civilizations. Scholars study its texts for academic purposes, exploring its historical and cultural contexts.

Ultimately, whether the Bible is considered the ultimate truth or not is a matter of personal and religious belief, and opinions may vary among individuals and religious sects. But those of Christian faith know it to be the true word of God.

57

CHAPTER FIFTEEN

NOTES

Are there different kinds of Christians?

Yes, there are true believers (Christians) and those who believe they are Christian but do not adhere to the Christian faith or God's word. Various denominations and branches within Christianity, result in different kinds of believers who may call themselves Christians. To be a follower of Christ is to believe that He died for the propitiation of our sins and three days later rose from the grave. To repent from your sins, confess your sins and ask His forgiveness, and have faith in Him, believing this to be true. As mentioned, the divisions of these different doctrines can be based on theological beliefs, interpretations of scripture, worship practices, organizational structures, and cultural factors. Below are some of the major Christian traditions and denominations:

Guile's of the Devil

CHAPTER SIXTEEN

NOTES

1. **Roman Catholicism:** The largest Christian denomination, with its center in Rome and led by the Pope. It places importance on the authority of the Pope, sacraments, and tradition and does not teach the Deity of Christ but puts the Pope on an equal level with God and the priests on an equal level with Christ, believing they have the power to absolve sin. And exact penance for the sins of the followers.

2. **Eastern Orthodoxy:** Comprising various autocephalous (self-governing) churches, primarily in Eastern Europe and the Middle East. It emphasizes liturgical worship, sacraments, and the authority of the Patriarchs.

3. **Protestantism:** A diverse group of Christian denominations that emerged from the Protestant Reformation in the 16th century. Some prominent Protestant denominations include:

- Lutheranism: Established by Martin Luther, focusing on justification by faith alone and the authority of scripture.

- Anglicanism: Originating from the Church of England, with a blend of Catholic and Reformed traditions.

- Baptist: Emphasizing baptism of believers, religious freedom, and local church autonomy.

- Presbyterian: Organized with representative assemblies and guided by the principles of governance outlined by John Calvin.

- Methodism: Influenced by John Wesley's teachings, emphasizing personal holiness and social justice.

- Pentecostalism: Emphasizing the gifts of the Holy Spirit, such as speaking in tongues, divine healing, Snake charming, forehead-slapping and various other methods...

4. **Non-denominational Christianity:** These are independent churches or individuals who do not align with a specific denomination, choosing to worship and practice their faith outside formal denominational structures. They believe that the bible is the true Word of God and generally teach the word in a book by book, chapter by chapter and verse by verse method.

Not deviating from the word of God. (informally falling in the protestant category).

This list is not exhaustive, and there are numerous other Christian traditions, denominations, and independent groups that exist worldwide. Within each denomination, there can also be variations in beliefs and practices among local congregations and individual believers. And the list keeps growing.

I heard this said once:

"The diversity within Christianity reflects the richness and complexity of the religion and the various ways in which people express their faith."

-Author unknown.

Although you may think this sounds right, it is not. This statement is far from the truth. It is one of Satan's subtle ways of getting believers to deviate from the truth of God's word. As a believer in Christ, there is only one way to heaven: Repentance to Jesus Christ, asking forgiveness for your sins, and accepting Him as your Lord and Savior, Faith in Jesus Christ, Believing He died for us, buried in a tomb for three days and rising (Resurrected) from the tomb!

To be strong and able to withstand the fiery darts, subtle distractions and deceptions Satan throws your way you need to read His word daily, strive to stay in His will; wear the full armor of God, pray to Him for strength, wisdom and to not be distracted by Satan.

Ultimately, it's our own sin nature that draws us away from God!

CHAPTER SEVENTEEN

How many denominations of Christianity are there?

NOTES

It is challenging to determine the exact number of denominations within Christianity due to the diverse and decentralized nature of the religion due in no small part from the doctrinal differences in man's faulty theology. The World Christian Encyclopedia, a comprehensive reference work on global Christianity, estimated that there were over 45,000 denominations worldwide as of 2021. However, it is important to note that this number includes various sub-denominations, independent churches, and distinct groups with theological and organizational differences.

It's worth mentioning that the classification of Christian groups into distinct denominations can sometimes be subjective and dependent on various factors, such as theological differences, organizational structures, and cultural contexts. Furthermore, the number of denominations can fluctuate over time as new groups emerge or existing groups merge or dissolve.

While the number of denominations can seem large, it is important to recognize that there are also significant areas of theological agreement and common beliefs among true Christians. Many denominations share core doctrines such as the belief in the Trinity, the divinity of Jesus Christ, and the importance of the Bible as sacred scripture.

Despite the diversity of denominations within Christianity, there are also efforts towards ecumenism, which seeks to foster unity and cooperation among different Christian traditions. **"Can you say one world religion?"**

71

CHAPTER EIGHTEEN

What keeps people from Christianity?

NOTES

There are various reasons why individuals may not adhere to or identify with Christianity. It's important to note that people's reasons for not embracing a particular religious belief can be highly personal and varied.

Here are some common factors that may contribute to someone not practicing or identifying as Christian:

1. **Different religious or spiritual beliefs:** People raised in a different religious tradition or have adopted different spiritual beliefs that are incompatible with Christianity.

2. **Lack of religious affiliation:** Some individuals may not have a strong religious affiliation or may identify as agnostic, atheist, or non-religious. They may not find sufficient evidence or personal conviction to believe in any particular religion, including Christianity.

3. **Philosophical or intellectual disagreements:** Some individuals may have philosophical or intellectual disagreements with certain Christian teachings or doctrines. They may find it challenging to reconcile their own worldview or rationality with aspects of Christian belief.

4. **Negative experiences or perceptions:** Past negative experiences with individuals or institutions associated with Christianity can influence someone's decision to distance themselves from the faith. This may include experiences of hypocrisy, judgment, or harm caused by people who identify as Christians.

5. **Cultural or societal factors:** Cultural or societal influences can also play a role. Some individuals may be part of communities or societies where Christianity is not the dominant or accepted belief system. Cultural, social, or family pressures may discourage or deter individuals from embracing Christianity.

6. **Lack of personal relevance or connection:** For some individuals, the teachings and practices of Christianity may not resonate with their personal experiences, needs, or values. They may not find it personally meaningful or relevant to their lives.

CHAPTER NINETEEN

What countries persecute Christianity?

NOTES

It's important to approach discussions about religion versus Jesus Christ with respect and understanding as people's beliefs and choices can be deeply personal and reflective of their unique experiences and perspectives. But the goal, and is in fact, a commission from God to all Christians, is to speak the truth of God's word. The Gospel of our Lord Jesus Christ.

Reflect on the truth of this statement

The true answer as to what keeps people from Christianity is SIN!

CHAPTER TWENTY

While religious persecution can occur in various parts of the world, it is important to note that the situation can change over time and can vary within different regions of a country. Here are a few examples of countries where instances of religious persecution against Christians have been reported: In other words, where Satan has a strong foothold.

NOTES

1. **North Korea:** The North Korean government has been reported to actively suppress and persecute Christians, considering them a threat to the regime. Christian worship is heavily regulated, and believers face severe penalties, including imprisonment, torture, and even execution.

2. **China:** While Christianity is officially recognized in China, there have been instances of religious persecution, particularly against unregistered or underground Christian communities. Churches have faced forced closures, cross removals, surveillance, and harassment by authorities, including murder and imprisonment. Chinese Communism is a direct threat to Christianity and any foreigner teaching Christianity in China will be put in prison for possibly years and may, in fact, face execution.

3. **Nigeria:** In certain parts of Nigeria, particularly in the northern regions, Christians have faced attacks from extremist groups, such as Boko Haram and Fulani militants. Churches have been targeted, and Christians have been subjected to violence, abduction, forced conversions and execution. This is not necessarily the country itself as a whole.

4. **Pakistan:** Christians in Pakistan have faced discrimination, social marginalization, and instances of violence. There have been reports of blasphemy accusations used as a means to target Christians, resulting in arrests, mob violence, and even death sentences.

5. **Eritrea (East Africa):** The Eritrean government has been known to restrict religious freedom, primarily for Christians. Unregistered churches are not recognized and face persecution, with reports of arrests, imprisonment, and torture of Christian believers.

6. **Iran:** Christians in Iran, particularly those from Muslim backgrounds who have converted to Christianity, have faced persecution and discrimination. Church gatherings are monitored, and converts risk legal penalties, social ostracism, and harassment by authorities. Even death.

Please note that this is not an exhaustive list, and there are instances of religious persecution against Christians in other countries as well. The severity and nature of persecution can vary, and it's crucial to rely on credible sources and reports for up-to-date and accurate information on the situation in specific regions or countries.

(In other words, do your research)

On the next page is a list of books of the bible with chapters and verses pertaining to Satan. It is not a complete list, but it's a start for your further study on the subject of Satan.

CHAPTER TWENTY-ONE

NOTES

1 Corinthians 7:5

5 Do not deprive each other except perhaps by mutual consent and for a time, so that you may devote yourselves to prayer. Then come together again so that Satan will not tempt you because of your lack of self-control.

1 John 3:8

8 The one who does what is sinful is of the devil because the devil has been sinning from the beginning. The reason the Son of God appeared was to destroy the devil's work.

2 Corinthians 11:3

3 But I am afraid that just as Eve was deceived by the serpent's cunning, your minds may somehow be led astray from your sincere and pure devotion to Christ.

Acts 5:3

3 Then Peter said, "Ananias, how is it that Satan has so filled your heart that you have lied to the Holy Spirit and have kept for yourself some of the money you received for the land?

John 8:44

44 You belong to your father, the devil, and you want to carry out your father's desires.

He was a murderer from the beginning, not holding to the truth, for there is no truth in him. When he lies, he speaks his native language, for he is a liar and the father of lies.

John 10:10

10 The thief comes only to steal and kill and destroy; I have come that they may have life, and have it to the full.

James 4:7

7 Submit yourselves, then, to God. Resist the devil, and he will flee from you.

NOTES

Matthew 16:23

23 Jesus turned and said to Peter, "Get behind me, Satan! You are a stumbling block to me; you do not have in mind the concerns of God, but merely human concerns."

Romans 16:20

20 The God of peace will soon crush Satan under your feet. The grace of our Lord Jesus be with you.

Zechariah 3:1-2

1 Then he showed me Joshua the high priest, standing before the angel of the LORD, and Satan standing at his right side to accuse him. **2** The LORD said to Satan, "The LORD rebuke you, Satan! The LORD, who has chosen Jerusalem, rebuke you! Is not this man a burning stick snatched from the fire?"

1 Peter 5:8-9

8 Be alert and of sober mind. Your enemy the devil prowls around like a roaring lion looking for someone to devour. **9** Resist him, standing firm in the faith, because you know that the family of believers throughout the world is undergoing the same kind of sufferings.

1 Corinthians 11:12-15

12 For as woman came from man, so also man is born of woman. But everything comes from God. **13** Judge for yourselves: Is it proper for a woman to pray to God with her head uncovered? **14** Does not the very nature of things teach you that if a man has long hair, it is a disgrace to him, **15** but that if a woman has long hair, it is her glory? For long hair is given to her as a covering.

NOTES

<u>Genesis 3:1-5</u>

1 Now the serpent was more crafty than any of the wild animals the LORD God had made. He said to the woman, "Did God really say, "You must not eat from any tree in the garden?" **2** The woman said to the serpent, "We may eat fruit from the trees in the garden, **3** but God did say, "You must not eat fruit from the tree that is in the middle of the garden, and you must not touch it, or you will die." **4** "You will not certainly die," the serpent said to the woman. **5** "For God knows that when you eat from it, your eyes will be opened, and you will be like God, knowing good and evil."

<u>Revelation 20:1-6</u>

1 And I saw an angel coming down out of heaven, having the key to the Abyss and holding in his hand a great chain. **2** He seized the dragon, that ancient serpent, who is the devil, or Satan, and bound him for a thousand years. **3** He threw him into the Abyss and locked and sealed it over him to keep him from deceiving the nations anymore until the thousand years were ended. After that, he must be set free for a short time. **4** I saw thrones on which were seated those who had been given authority to judge. And I saw the souls of those who had been beheaded because of their testimony about Jesus and because of the word of God. They had not worshiped the beast or its image and had not received its mark on their foreheads or their hands. They came to life and reigned with Christ a thousand years. **5** (The rest of the dead did not come to life until the thousand years were ended.) This is the first resurrection. **6** Blessed and holy are those who share in the first resurrection. The second death has no power over them, but they will be priests of God and of Christ and will reign with him for a thousand years.

NOTES

Ephesians 6:11-16

11 Put on the full armor of God, so that you can take your stand against the devil's schemes. **12** For our struggle is not against flesh and blood, but against the rulers, against the authorities, against the powers of this dark world and against the spiritual forces of evil in the heavenly realms. **13** Therefore put on the full armor of God, so that when the day of evil comes, you may be able to stand your ground, and after you have done everything, to stand. **14** Stand firm then, with the belt of truth buckled around your waist, with the breastplate of righteousness in place, **15** and with your feet fitted with the readiness that comes from the gospel of peace. **16** In addition to all this, take up the shield of faith, with which you can extinguish all the flaming arrows of the evil one.

Luke 22:1-6

1 Now the Festival of Unleavened Bread, called the Passover, was approaching, **2** and the chief priests and the teachers of the law were looking for some way to get rid of Jesus, for they were afraid of the people. **3** Then Satan entered Judas, called Iscariot, one of the Twelve. **4** And Judas went to the chief priests and the officers of the temple guard and discussed with them how he might betray Jesus. **5** They were delighted and agreed to give him money. **6** He consented, and watched for an opportunity to hand Jesus over to them when no crowd was present.

Job 1:6-12

6 One day the angels came to present themselves before the LORD, and Satan also came with them. **7** The LORD said to Satan, "Where have you come from?" Satan answered the LORD, "From roaming throughout the earth, going back and forth on it." **8** Then the LORD said to Satan, "Have you considered my servant Job? There is no one on earth like him; he is blameless and upright, a man who fears God and shuns evil." **9** "Does Job fear God for nothing?" Satan replied. **10** "Have you not put a hedge around him and his household and everything he has? You have blessed the work of his hands so that his flocks and herds are spread throughout the land. **11** But now stretch out your hand and strike everything he has, and he will surely curse you to your face." **12** The LORD said to Satan, "Very well, then, everything he has is in your power, but on the man himself do not lay a finger." Then Satan went out from the presence of the LORD.

NOTES

2 Corinthians 2:5-11

5 If anyone has caused grief, he has not so much grieved me as he has grieved all of you to some extent, not to put it too severely. **6** The punishment inflicted on him by the majority is sufficient. **7** Now, instead, you ought to forgive and comfort him, so that he will not be overwhelmed by excessive sorrow. **8** I urge you, therefore, to reaffirm your love for him. **9** Another reason I wrote you was to see if you would stand the test and be obedient in everything. **10** Anyone you forgive, I also forgive. And what I have forgiven —if there was anything to forgive, I have forgiven in the sight of Christ for your sake, **11** in order that Satan might not outwit us. For we are not unaware of his schemes.

2 Corinthians 12:1-10

1 I must go on boasting. Though there is nothing to be gained by it, I will go on to visions and revelations of the Lord. **2** I know a man in Christ who fourteen years ago was caught up to the third heaven—whether in the body or out of the body I do not know, God knows. **3** And I know that this man was caught up into paradise—whether in the body or out of the body I do not know, God knows— **4** and he heard things that cannot be told, which man may not utter. **5** On behalf of this man I will boast, but on my own behalf I will not boast, except of my weaknesses— **6** though if I should wish to boast, I would not be a fool, for I would be speaking the truth; but I refrain from it, so that no one may think more of me than he sees in me or hears from me. **7** So to keep me from becoming conceited because of the surpassing greatness of the revelations, a thorn was given me in the flesh, a messenger of Satan to harass me, to keep me from becoming conceited. **8** Three times I pleaded with the Lord about this, that it should leave me. **9** But he said to me, "My grace is sufficient for you, for my power is made perfect in weakness." Therefore I will boast all the more gladly of my weaknesses, so that the power of Christ may rest upon me. **10** For the sake of Christ, then, I am content with weaknesses, insults, hardships, persecutions, and calamities. For when I am weak, then I am strong.

There are many more scriptures pertaining to Satan, look them up. Read the word daily. Pray for wisdom to understand what you are read.

NOTES

About The Author

TM Brooks left home at the young age of twelve to start his life as an adventurer traveling around the country with Ringling Brothers & Barnum & Bailey Circus and the world doing what he did best, being him.. He held many positions while he worked at RB&BB circus. He worked as an animal handler, Wardrobe Specialist under Smitty for the entertainers and for a short time as a substitute catcher on the trapeze. He spent time as a logger in Montana, a cowhand in the same state, truck driver for a part of his life and too many other adventures to list TM Brooks has been following The Lord since he met who would become his wife of 32 years and the woman who led him to Christ. During those years we spent following Christ and serving Him. There were times on my part where that was a very difficult path but I have a very forgiving God and realized His Grace is enough. My purpose now is to try and lead those who don't know our Lord & Savior to His saving Grace. I believe that only by knowing Him you can truly know the meaning of unconditional love and peace.